HARRY
at the Doctors

written by Ruby Nelson
Illustrated by Danny Noonan

The views and opinions expressed in this book are solely those of the author and do not reflect the views or opinions of the author.

Harry at the Doctors - Copyright © 2024 Ruby Nelson

ISBN: 978-1-922664-83-9 (Paperback) 978-1-922664-84-6 (Hardback)
All rights reserved. Neither this book nor any parts within it may be sold or reproduced in any format by any electronic or mechanical means, including information storage and retrieval systems without permission in writing from the author. The only exception is by a reviewer, who may quote short excerpts in a review.

Harry and Teddy were snuggled under their blankets, feeling tired and sniffly. Their noses were stuffy, and their throats felt scratchy.

"Come on, sleepyheads," called Mommy with a gentle smile. "We have an appointment with Dr, John!"

Harry groaned, pulling the blanket over his head. "I don't feel like getting out of bed."

Mommy sat down next to Harry. "I know you don't feel great, but Dr. John will help. Let's get dressed and ready to go."

With a little help, Harry wriggled into his clothes and was snug and warm. He made his way down the stairs and out to the car. Poor Teddy wasn't feeling very well either.

"Safety first!" said Mommy, clicking their seatbelts into place.

"Always!" Harry chimed in, though he still looked a little sleepy.

On the way to the doctor's office, Mommy handed Harry some tissues. "Blow your nose so you can breathe a little easier darling," she said.

"I think we are almost here Mommy" said Harry as he pointed towards the medical centre.

Inside, a kind lady at the front desk greeted them. "Hello, Harry and Teddy! Dr. John will see you soon. You can wait over there."

Harry and Teddy settled into the waiting room. Harry spotted a familiar book. "Look, Teddy! It's our favorite dino book!"

Harry flipped through the pages, giggling at the pictures, until a cheerful voice called out, "Harry and Teddy! It's nice to see you!"

Dr. John had a big smile and a warm voice. "How are my favorite little patients today?"

Harry followed him into the exam room. "Let's see how you're feeling," Dr. John said as he washed his hands. "Harry, you're up first!"

"Harry, can you show me on Teddy where you are feeling sore?" said Dr.John.

"I'm feeling sore in my throat and I feel a little hot just here" said Harry.

"I'm going to check your throat, ears and check your temperature . Is that OK?" said Dr. John.

Dr. John used a little paddle that helped keep Harry's tongue down so he could look at the back of Harry's mouth. "Yes, I can see some redness in there", said Dr. John.

"I'm now going to look into your ears and also check your temperature." said Dr.John "This will help me find out why you are feeling unwell".

"Hmm," Dr. John said thoughtfully. "It looks like you've caught a cold. But the good news is, with some rest and water, you'll feel better very soon!"

Harry's eyes brightened. "Really?"

"Really," Dr. John assured him. "Just give it a day or two."

"Thank you, Dr. John," said Harry with a big smile.

Teddy had his turn next, and Dr. John said the same thing: "Rest, water, and time will do the trick Teddy!"

By the time they left, Harry was already feeling a little better just knowing he was on the mend.

The next day, the sniffles started to go away, and Harry was back to his usual playful self.

"Mommy, let's go to the park!" Harry called out.

"Sounds like my boy is all better!" Mommy said with a laugh.

And he was — just as Dr. John had promised!

HARRY'S Book Series

Available Via all Major Online Bookstores

www.ingramcontent.com/pod-product-compliance
Lightning Source LLC
LaVergne TN
LVHW070219080526
838202LV00067B/6854